W9-BDO-236

Good Food

I Like Pasta

By Jennifer Julius

Children's Press
A Division of Grolier Publishing
New York / London / Hong Kong / Sydney
Danbury, Connecticut

Photo Credits: Cover, 5, 7, 9, 11, 13, 15, 17, 21 by Maura Boruchow; p. 19 © IndexStock Photography, Inc.

Contributing Editor: Jennifer Ceaser
Book Design: Nelson Sa

Library of Congress Cataloging-in-Publication Data

Julius, Jennifer.
I like pasta / by Jennifer Julius.
p. cm. – (Good food)
Includes bibliographical references and index.
ISBN 0-516-23132-4 (lib. bdg.) – ISBN 0-516-23057-3 (pbk.)
1. Cookery (Pasta)—Juvenile literature. [1. Pasta products.] I. Title. II. Series.

TX809.M17 J85 2000
641.8'22—dc21

00-043067

Copyright © 2001 by Rosen Book Works, Inc.
All rights reserved. Published simultaneously in Canada.
Printed in China
8 9 10 R 11 10 62

Contents

1	Spaghetti	6
2	Ravioli	8
3	Lasagna	10
4	Macaroni	12
5	New Words	22
6	To Find Out More	23
7	Index	24
8	About the Author	24

I like pasta.

Do you like pasta?

Pasta comes in all
shapes and sizes.

This pasta is long and thin.

It looks like strings.

It is spaghetti (speh-**geh**-tee).

This pasta is square.

It is filled with cheese.

It is ravioli (ra-vee-**oh**-lee).

This pasta is **flat**.

The edges are **wavy**.

It is lasagna (leh-**zah**-nyah).

This pasta is shaped like an **elbow**.

I eat it with cheese.

It is macaroni (mak-eh-**roh**-nee).

This pasta looks like
a butterfly.

It is bow tie pasta!

This pasta is shaped like a shell.

It has cheese inside.

I eat the pasta with tomato **sauce**.

All pasta is made from **dough**.

Flour, salt, and eggs make dough.

What kind of pasta do you like to eat?

New Words

dough (**doh**) a mix of flour, salt, and eggs

elbow (**el**-boh) the part of your body where your arm bends

flat (**flat**) smooth and even

sauce (**saws**) something poured over food

wavy (**way**-vee) bending like a wave